PRAISE FOR
JUST AS YOU ARE

"Lisa Fahey ministers to her husband, daughters, family, friends, community and country by speaking truth and expressing the heart of Jesus through her actions to all generations. She is real. She models the heart of Jesus as she has met Him personally through real-life experiences of both trials and celebrations. This Bible Study captures your attention and heart with real-life stories that will draw you closer to your Heavenly Father."

Tylee Peterson

"Lisa truly speaks to my heart on surrendering to the trust of God's plan for my life. A bold and compelling witness of authentic love between two people, but ultimately between God and His beloved."

Jill Patten

PRAISE FOR *JUST AS YOU ARE*

"Catherine of Sienna said, 'Be who God meant you to be, and you will set the world on fire.' Lisa Fahey has done that, and she uses the fire to illuminate the way for her readers in her new book, *Just As You Are*. Lisa's gentle spirit shines through as she recounts how God brought her through a difficult time, taught her to trust, and ultimately, to realize that He had given her these experiences so that she might share them, no matter how much that scared her. This book will make you ask, 'What have I been doing with the life God has given *me*?'"

Mary Ann Koenig
Bible Study Leader

"Lisa's book captures the heart of storytelling and its essential role in evangelization. She weaves practical tips with her own witness to seamlessly demonstrate how our stories of encounter with God can bring others to conversion. Most importantly, the kerygma (the core Gospel message) forms the backbone of her suggestions—encouraging readers to keep each witness and testimony centered, not on ourselves, but on Jesus' paschal mystery."

Kristin Bird
Executive Director Burning Hearts Disciples

"Lisa Fahey shares vulnerable stories from her heart of the many ways God has made Himself known to her through all of life's moments including death and daring decisions to pray for the grace to act upon His will. The reader can hear the gentleness of Lisa's voice as she takes us on the up-and-down journey of her life with Christ and encourages us toward our own authentic relationship with Jesus through prayer and reflection."

Chika Anyanwu
Author of My Encounter: How I Met Jesus In Prayer

"Lisa's book, *Just As You Are*, draws you into a place of transparency, honesty, and vulnerability. Lisa has a way of crafting story in such a way that you feel as if you were a bystander placed in the narrative of her book. It is an invitation to reflect on how God's story has been at work in the narrative of your own personal journey!"

Dave Kinsman
Author of Hope Has Arrived

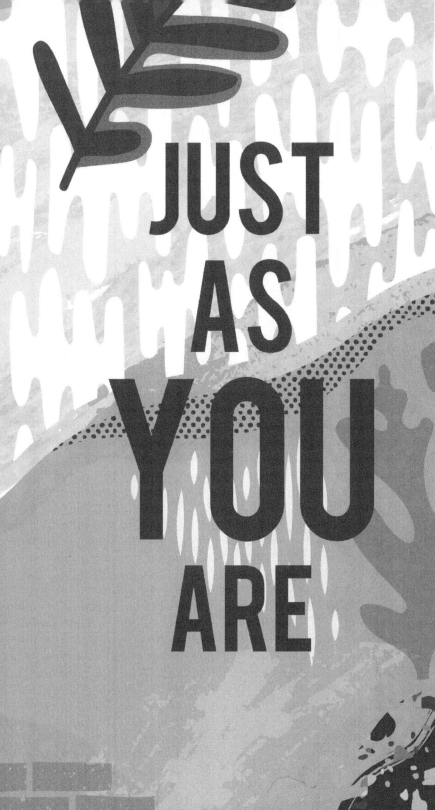

LISA FAHEY

JUST AS YOU ARE

THRONE
PUBLISHING GROUP

How Your Testimony Can Impact People
In Ways You Never Thought Possible

Throne Publishing Group
2329 N. Career Ave #215
Sioux Falls, SD 57107
ThronePG.com

TABLE OF CONTENTS

PART ONE
EXPERIENCING

Chapter One
My Story

As I wrestle with what I am going to share with you, I want you to know that I too was not prepared for the chapter in my life following my high school graduation. My story consists of a young man by the name of Shane, and his story of how he had visions of future events. These were not visions of future dreams and plans, but instead were visions of actual events that would later take place. I should forewarn you that this is not an ordinary story and likely one that you, like I, have never encountered before. To gain some perspective on the story of Shane and I, it is important to first give you some understanding of the beginning chapters of my life.

My childhood could be best described as encompassed with love and surrounded by family. My grandparents, aunts, uncles and cousins all lived within a twenty-mile radius of my family's farm. My memories as a little girl revolved around feeling safe, nurtured, and encouraged. Of all my family members, there were three who played a pivotal role in my life and in my walk with Jesus; my Grandma Regina, Sister Anna Rose, and Verena.

Just As You Are

I grew up in one of those small towns where people watched out for one another and half the town knew the trouble you were going to get into before you even thought about doing it. I loved our tightly knit community and being involved in the church, town events, and extracurricular activities. It wasn't until the death of my grandpa that things started to change and my family struggled to find their way to happiness. I noticed the sadness of my father and grandmother and I longed to have them happy again.

When I was in middle school, my dad began driving a truck and would be on the road from Sunday to Friday. My life had completely changed from what it had been when I was a little girl and we became what is now the typical modern family; all going in different directions. This was my life through the rest of my middle and high school years.

As time drew closer to my graduating, I still had no idea what I was going to do next. I knew I wanted to attend college but I wasn't sure how I was going to afford it. Just a few months before graduation, my Uncle Leo came by the house and talked with my parents about a possible job opportunity for me. He said he knew I had been looking at going to college and had found a summer job at a tourist stop working for a local family and their three businesses. I was so excited for the opportunity but scared at the thought, of being away from home for the first time. Only a few days after graduation, I left my hometown and was on my way to start my new job.

My Story

My first night away from home, my Uncle Leo took me to a rodeo where he introduced me to a cowboy named Shane. I learned that Shane was the son of the couple who owned the business I would be working at that summer. The following day, Shane came by to give me a ride to my new job. A short couple of days later, he asked me to go on a date with him. On our first date, Shane took the longer route home as he shared about himself and his life. What he shared with me made it a night I would never forget.

Shane explained that during his sophomore year in high school, he had a vision. He had been working with his dad and brother on the ranch and as he was walking towards his parent's house, he felt excruciating pain throbbing throughout his head. Shane said he fell to his knees. His mother had seen him collapse from the house and ran out to him. He then began to describe the gruesome plane crash that had played out in his mind, with human body parts splayed in every direction around the scene of the crash. Shane had never experienced anything like this before and was confused about what had just happened; what he had seen. His family had their pastor come out to pray with them. While he was there, the pastor told them of a horrific plane crash at Chicago O'Hare airport that he had seen on the news. The details of the crash aligned perfectly with those in Shane's vision.

I sat there bewildered by what Shane had just shared with me. I wondered, 'how do you begin to even process

married. After spending the rest of Christmas break on our honeymoon, we returned to school and each graduated in May of that year.

After college, Shane and I were in a partnership of farming and ranching with both his brother and sister-in-law, and his dad and mom. At this time I worked at a law firm twenty-miles from the ranch, and our lives were taking shape as a young couple in the adult world. That fall, my brother would be coming home after being in service overseas, so I made plans to go back home to see him. Shane had some friends planning to come out and hunt with him, so he decided to stay behind at the ranch. While I was gone, I was anxious and would call home often to check in on him, but he would always be okay. When I returned a few days later, I walked in to find Shane sitting in the hallway on the floor of our house. When I asked him what he was doing, he said he had been out in the barn when he felt as though two people were there walking with him; one of the people being his deceased grandpa and the other being an angel. In my discomfort, I told him I didn't know what to do when he had these visions, and left him sitting there to go make supper.

It was about a month and a half following our second anniversary that our story shifted. I had been ill and was hospitalized for a couple of days. The impact of being sick caused Shane great concern and sadness. He got home the first night after visiting me and was upset so he went to visit with his folks. He told them

My Story

he didn't know what he would do if something were to happen to me.

One morning as I was watching the news and drinking coffee, I noticed Shane standing in the doorway. He was going to feed the calves in the feedlot but instead of heading out, he stood in the doorway staring at me for quite a while. I became confused and self-conscious. It felt as if he knew something and I became uncomfortable in the silence. I asked Shane if he needed anything or if there was something wrong. He responded that he had wanted to look at me one more time. Then Shane told me he loved me and advised me to be careful. Shane told me that he, his dad, and his brother would be sorting calves for an upcoming sale. As I was pulling out of the driveway to go to work, I observed Shane in the tractor. He saw me and put his hand up to wave goodbye. The way he had waved at me was odd enough to bring me to pray for him and I asked God to let Shane know I would be okay.

After I arrived at the law firm where I was working at the time, I went through my pile of work and noticed a complaint that needed the sheriff's signature. When I called the sheriff's office, the secretary had informed me that the sheriff was not there. She said that he was on his way to the ranch because there had been a horse accident and an ambulance was also on its way. I asked her if she knew who was hurt and she told me she didn't know. With both my mother-in-law and sister-in-law traveling, there was no one to answer my calls or to tell me what was happening. I went into my boss's office to tell him about the horse accident, and that I needed to go to the hospital. As I headed to my car, I fearfully began to think about Shane's vision and wondered if it was coming to fruition.

As I was driving to the hospital, I saw the ambulance coming my direction. I pulled over in hopes they would stop and let me join them however they did not slow down. I traveled behind but soon the ambulance was out of my sight. I was scared and began to pray aloud as tears ran down my cheeks. I kept trying to reassure myself that Shane was not the one injured. A few miles from the hospital, I saw a bright ball of light come up from the valley where the town was located and went over my car and some round bales of hay. My immediate response was *oh no, he is gone!* Then I reassured myself that I didn't know that for sure and continued to pray. A few minutes later, the sheriff's car passed me and I recognized the passengers as Shane's dad and brother. My heart was fluttering with anxiety and fear.

Shane's brother met me at the door and informed me that while they were sorting the calves Shane's horse slipped and fell on top of him. Although they didn't know exactly what had cause the slip, they suspected the horse had hit some ice on the ground. His brother explained that Shane had not been breathing so their dad gone to the house to call the ambulance. In the meantime Shane began to breathe.

My Story

His brother assured me that Shane was going to be okay. We had been in the waiting room for a while when the doctor came in and told us that Shane had died; there was nothing more he could do for him. I remember Shane's dad and brother asked me if I wanted to see him. They were on each side of me. Across from the waiting room, there was a highway patrolman standing at the nurse's station. I remember he was looking down and had a sad look on his face. I was in shock not knowing what to expect when I saw Shane. Once in the room, all I remember is how peaceful Shane looked. The first thought that came to my mind was that as difficult a decision as it would be, if Shane could choose between Jesus or me, he would choose Jesus.

A good friend of the family's came by to drive me home. As we reached the exit to the road we lived on, I remember staring off at the ranch, as God placed on my heart that this chapter of my story was done but there would be many more chapters left to come. He once again assured me that He would be with me.

The days leading to the funeral were full of the support from many relatives and friends who would call or stop by to be with us. The funeral for Shane was so big that it was moved to the community center. On the day of his funeral, I wanted to take one more look at Shane before they closed the casket. I remember wanting to touch his hand and when I had, I was startled by how cold it was. As they closed the casket, reality began to set in that I would never see him again.

Just As You Are

I stayed with family in the days following the funeral. It was difficult to be there since my home was back at the ranch. I kept waiting for the phone to ring in hopes it would be Shane checking up on me or to wake up and find that this was all just a bad dream.

After a few days I went back to the ranch and although I was happy to be in my home again, I also was scared to be alone. It was hard to not have Shane around so I found a couple of books to read to help me with my grief. According to the books, there would be a lot of firsts to overcome since Shane's death. The very first night back in our home, I was scared to shut the lights off so all of them were on except those in my bedroom. If I couldn't sleep in the middle of the night, I would grab Shane's Bible and read until I fell asleep again. My life was forever changed and I wondered what God had planned for me.

In looking back at this time of my life, I have recognized that God was with Shane and I in everything. I have often wondered why my Uncle Leo felt called to find summer employment for me. Two years ago, I asked him just that. His response was that he didn't know. What I do know is God can do whatever He wants and He can orchestrate people and circumstances in our life. Even though Shane was a faith-filled man, he was able to share his struggles and concerns, and his confidence was in God who would give him the strength he needed. By his example I, too, learned about trusting God in all things. Because I stepped outside of my comfort zone as a young adult, I soon found there was something bigger than myself and it was far more than I could have imagined.

I remember that one day as we were heading home from church, I told Shane that I felt bad about the relationship I had with a family member. When he asked if I had confessed it I told him that I had but I was still feeling guilty. It was then he said to me, "Lisa, it is a bigger sin to not believe in God's love and mercy for you, than the actual sin you confessed." His words stunned me with conviction and we sat in silence for the rest of the ride home as I reflected on what he had said.

What I learned from my experience with Shane is that no matter how young or old you are, God invites us to have a life changing encounter with Him, and my life and faith have not been the same since I met that man the night of the rodeo.

Life can be challenging, but we are never alone. Jesus is more than we can imagine, and He cares for us in our everyday lives. Just as with Shane's second vision of a light coming towards him and the testimony that Jesus was with him, you and I can be confident that He is with us, too. I had often thought that Jesus was out of reach for me but there is more to experience in your life when you have a personal relationship with Jesus.

So where does a person go after a life changing experience? I want to leave you with this thought; 'Jesus will be with you.' No matter the chapter you are currently in of your life's story, just know He loves you and cares for you. Are you ready to dive into experiencing this kind of love and faith? Remember, there are more chapters to your life and God will be with you no matter where He takes you.

Reflection Questions

Question #1: How do Shane's experiences encourage you to open your mind about how Jesus can talk to us?

Question #2: How has God been with you through tough times, as He was with me when Shane passed?

Question #3: How did you stay close to God during times of difficulty? What kept you close to Him and how did you see Him show up in your life?

Chapter Two
Making The Move

It didn't take me long before I realized I needed to be busy and around people. In the summer following Shane's death, I decided to go back to college. There were so many firsts I had to tackle now that I had lost Shane. One of those firsts was to date again. As awkward as I felt about dating again, I also felt a sense of peace. I eventually met a man named Pat and although I was interested in him, I wasn't sure what to think about the feelings I had for him. There was this tug-of-war in my heart; with the love I still had for Shane and the thought of loving someone else. After discernment and prayer, I felt at peace with my new feelings and was finally able to love someone else as I had once loved Shane.

After Pat and I married, we moved to the same area as Pat's father, stepmom, sister and family; we were happy and enjoying life as a young married couple. About two years later, we found out we were going to have a baby. I was nervous about this pregnancy as I had miscarried Shane's baby the summer before he died. Because of this, Pat and I waited on sharing the news until after the first trimester. Our baby girl Alisha was born on a stormy winter day. She was absolutely beautiful at 6 lbs. and 10 ounces. She was petite and when we would hold her she would scrunch her little body into a small ball. We were afraid she was suffocating and would have to constantly reposition ourselves as she snuggled in our arms. Alisha was up at night and would sleep in the morning. She was a fun toddler who was confident and outgoing. Two years later we had another beautiful daughter that we named Rebecca who came into the world at 8 lbs. and 12 ounces. Pat's Grandma, Minnie, had told us she always wanted a girl with the name Rebecca. The night she was born, the nurses brought Rebecca in for a feeding. She snuggled into me and I was so mesmerized by her sweetness that I didn't ring for the nurses to come back and get her. Even though we had the typical sleepless nights, teething, colds, and other common issues we were smitten by our girls and loved being their parents. I had the privilege to be a stay at home mom. It was a dream come true for me. To help with finances I was self-employed in cosmetic sales. I would work when Pat was home from his shift or when the girls were napping. We were the typical family working and watching our daughters grow up.

During this season of my life, my walk with Jesus had been a routine of going to church on the weekend and to pray as needed. However, my walk with Jesus grew, because of the advice of Mary Kay Ash. Our girls were two and four years old at the time. I had earned a free car and had just finished up qualifications as a sales director. I went to a training conference and the owner of the company Mary Kay Ash, encouraged all of us to arise early in the morning to spend the first part of the day with God. She promised us that when we gave God the first part of our day we would start off in the right direction. This was not always easy with two little ones, so I began slowly by setting my alarm fifteen minutes early before the girls woke up. I had my cup of coffee in one hand and a daily devotional in the other. It took a couple of weeks, but I am here to say, that I enjoyed the peace and quiet with Jesus. This time alone with Him became the best part of my morning. After spending time in the morning with Jesus, I soon found myself listening to Contemporary Christian music on my computer as I worked in my home office.

After sixteen years in our first home, my husband had an opportunity to apply for a promotion. However, if he got the promotion we would have to move. We talked about the advantages and disadvantages. I told Pat that I would pray for God's guidance on what to do. Because of my new experiences with prayer and listening to worship music, my heart had been inclined to go ask God for guidance. I used to ask God to bless my decision after the fact but never in the questioning of if we should do something. When I prayed this time it was different; I was seeking Him to help us do His Will. If we were to stay behind, we would be good with it. But if we were to go, we would be obedient. This was so new to me. Pat and I were concerned for the girls and how they would adjust to their new home and school. We also wondered if this would financially be a good decision.

I felt peace and that God was calling us to move. Pat received the promotion and left a couple days after 9/11. The girls and I stayed behind so that they could continue with school and I could begin getting things ready to move. Saying goodbye to all the memories we had made of our family, friends, and our first home began to set in. We all experienced a rollercoaster of emotions. It was definitely hard to say goodbye to the sixteen years we had spent here building our life together.

As we drove away from our home, I felt excitement that there was something new around the corner. I glanced up as we were driving away and looked in my rear view mirror at the girls and the town we had called home. I begin to tear up as I thought about the uncertainty of things ahead for us but the closer, we got to our new location, I couldn't help but feel we were at home. Following the will of God and moving to this new location seemed like the most natural thing we did. Despite our fears and worries, we felt at peace and knew we could walk in faith on our new adventure.

The first year following our move was a whirlwind. Everyone seemed to have transitioned to our new life and home with ease. God placed us among some great neighbors. I became friends with Amy, a neighbor who lived across the street from me. Amy would talk about her women's Bible study she was involved in.

Making The Move

I had always wanted to know how to study the Bible and had such a desire to begin. I began to pray and asked God to put it on Amy's heart to invite me to their next study.

God answered my prayer. One day Amy stopped by and asked me if I would like to join the group. I was so delighted that I began shopping for my first Bible. God was moving in my life. I just had no idea what His plans were and what He would be doing to my heart.

I was so excited about what was to come that I couldn't sleep the night before my first bible study. I was honest with the group that I had never studied the Bible before. The women encouraged and helped me as we reviewed the study each week. I would wake up early in the morning, grab a cup of coffee and begin to dive into the homework for the upcoming week's lessons. I was beginning to develop a hunger for God and His Word.

I enjoyed learning about God's Word and listening to the conversations among the women. My prayer time became fuller and I found myself asking God questions to the things I didn't understand. Not all questions had an answer, but there were times the answers would be revealed in the Scriptures.

At the end of each one of our study sessions, we would share prayer intentions. Praying for others opened up my heart to see people differently. My heart was open to change and to serve others. It was during this time I attended a workshop and learned that our subliminal conscience is like a sponge. We are to be careful with what we feed our minds. One quote given at the workshop was "what you think about, you will bring about". At home we began applying this strategy to the way we lived our everyday lives. We filtered the shows on TV and the movies we watched. The only music playing in the car or at home was Contemporary Christian music. We were feeding our conscience with Christ.

My heart was on fire for Christ and my family had noticed. I was happier and seemed to take life at a calmer pace. As the obstacles of life came our way, I was at peace. Instead of my first responses to difficult situations being one of panic, fear, impatience or worry, I would instead go to the Lord in prayer and trust that He would provide for us. Which meant I was calmer in the trials and struggles. Because I was calmer, the reactions of my family were calmer as well. I began to notice God was working things out for our good. Sometimes at the dinner table, our conversations were about what I was learning in my Bible studies. There was a light that had been sparked and was quickly turning into a flame.

In reflecting on my life prior to the move, I tried to do most things on my own. I am an introvert at heart so opening myself up to others was not an easy process. I soon trusted the women of my group and recognized the value of community. Community had renewed me and I realized that the women in my group had struggles in their lives as well. Life had become easier having others to share and pray with.

The Word renewed me in establishing the habit of memorizing Scriptures to help me in any daily struggles my family or I would encounter. In doing this one simple exercise of saying the memorized verse out loud, I was reminded God had the power and I could count on Him with His Word. I soon trusted in God's presence in my life, and recognized how He loved me and my family. My prayer life became a dialogue with God. No longer did I pray a Hail Mary pass for last minute assistance or His blessing. I was confident I could trust in Him and go to Him with everything.

I want to encourage you to have this type of confidence in God. The first step in building a relationship with Him is through prayer. It is as simple as having a conversation with God and listening for His response. Another way that you can build your trust in God is by reading His promises in the Bible. I will be talking more about God's Word and how you can study God's Word more effectively later in this book. Are you ready for your life to change for the better? All you will need is a willing heart.

Reflection Questions

Question #1: When did God lead you outside of your comfort zone and what did He do in your life as you stepped out in faith?

Question #2: Is God calling you out of a comfort zone right now? How is He doing this? What is holding you back from your step of faith?

Question #3: As you step out, what is a verse you could commit to memory to help you during times of uncertainty?

PART TWO
TRANSFORMING

Chapter Three
Let God Do His Work

God is a God of order; therefore God is the creator of time. Could you imagine what life would feel like if everything happened all at once? God creates time for our benefit. How we define time and how God defines time are completely different. Here is an example of God's timing; "Do not ignore this one fact beloved that with the Lord one day is like a thousand years and a thousand years like one day." (2 Peter 3:8) We measure time by how long a person lives, whereas God defines time as ordered and planned for His purpose and the Kingdom calendar.

Every day we make the decision to either waste time or to use our time wisely. Most often we tend to take for granted the time we have been given. When something traumatic happens, time seems to stop. When I was twenty-two years old, I experienced time stopping as the result of Shane's death. Because of this one event, a permanent mark was put on my life as time had come to a stop. From this life experience, I learned the value of time and how to use it wisely.

Time seems to go by faster the older a person becomes.

Just As You Are

In looking back, you begin to see the culmination of experiences over the days and years of one's life. We are astounded as we look back and see all that has taken place during a lifespan. It is as if you are thumbing through a book from the back cover to the beginning of the book. As you look through the chapters, you see defining moments in one's life and how God was working things out in each chapter. As you are living these moments, it was hard to see Him or that anything good could come from it. One thing is for certain; the more chapters you have, the more stories of faith you will have to share.

Time is fleeting. Seasons come and seasons go. There is a constant movement of change. In today's culture, we have adapted to fast food, fast access to information, and fast results. Therefore, when it comes to waiting, our patience is short. We have grown accustomed to quick results and resolve.

Our hearts are hungry and we find ourselves unsatisfied. The desire to acquire or grasp for things is a constant temptation to us. We are no different than Adam and Eve in wanting things our way and wanting them now.

The desire to want more and to have it instantly can leave one feeling restless. The only fix for this restlessness is Jesus. Jesus is the only one who can fill the hole of our restless hearts. In The Confessions of Saint Augustine of Hippo, he quotes "our hearts are restless until we rest in you."

Let God Do His Work

God doesn't operate in the mentality of instant gratification or fixes. All time and seasons are ordained by God. We cannot control God or what goes on around us. God the Creator began time and time is in His control. God is omniscient and He has set into motion His plan for eternity.

In our circumstances, God uses time to His advantage in working things out for the good (Romans 8:28). Our tendency is to desire an instant fix or quick solution however, it is in the waiting one begins to grow in their relationship with God. It's as if God is strengthening our spiritual muscles so that we may have the strength to persevere.

The beauty of God is that not one situation is wasted. It is through time, circumstances and others that He turns us back to Him. To God every soul is important and worth saving. "The Lord is not slow in keeping his promise, as some understand slowness. Instead he is patient with us, not wanting anyone to perish, but everyone to come to repentance" (2 Peter 3:9).

Have you ever heard of the saying be careful for what you pray for? This is so true. I remember once asking God for more patience. The answer came in real time with people who would cut in front of me in traffic or in the coffee shop. Or the store clerk whose cash register was acting up. When I asked Him, many opportunities came up to help me exercise my patience. It was times like these that I knew I would need to breathe in Christ and exhale me and my weaknesses.

Resiliency

When you are resilient and persevere, others look to you and your message as a sign of encouragement. The trials and struggles of this life, can be exhausting when you try to navigate it on your own. Everyone has a moment when they have reached their capacity and all that is left is to let go or let God. It is as if God is saying *why are you holding on so tight? Just rest in me for I am here for you.* It doesn't mean we are to quit, it just means to allow God in so that His glory can shine through. God steps in to our lives when we are at the end of our ropes as if to say *here let me help you with this.* It is at these moments God says great, you are where I need you to be resting in my arms. To rest is not only in the physical sense but the ability to surrender total control and allow God to come in and take over. Often times after I have exhausted all my means, it is when God says, *Come daughter it is time to let me take over.* So how does one rest you may ask? Look to the example Jesus gave us. "But Jesus often withdrew to lonely places and prayed." (Luke 5:16). Jesus showed us the way to rest and surrender all we are and all we have to do is go to the Father.

In my late thirties I had a desire to study the Bible. I remember this one desire as a turning point in my life. If you recall, I admitted that I had not studied the Bible before and was embarrassed in that admission. I had been teaching youth and children for years about the faith, however when it came to Scripture,

Let God Do His Work

I had no idea. Time was passing and my desire was strong to get in the Word of God. I was open and gave God permission to do His work in me.

Sometimes I find myself wanting to skip over a lesson the Lord had for me because it was hard to surrender to His perfect will. Some of the examples I can think of today are my loved ones, hopes, worries, plans, concerns, etc. This is when I notice that His timing seems to be slower than I want it to be. It is at these times I am looking for a quick fix or response from God. It is in the waiting for God's timing that bears much fruit. "God's timing teaches us, so we may gain wisdom" (Psalm 90:12).

We would not grow our spiritual muscles if God would come in and instantly fix things for us. It is in His timing we grow in wisdom and understanding. Sometimes, it is in our mistakes that we can learn the most. God is forming you and teaching you, all that is required is courage to allow Him to do so and to keep pressing in.

A Changed Heart

God's best work in us will require a changed heart. Our hearts reveal much about ourselves whether it is caught up in the worldly things or of God. "Where the heart is so is your treasure." (Matthew 6:21) Is your heart ready to receive the good things He has for you? When you trust God, you are giving Him permission to do what He wants through you. To surrender your will is to say *Lord, I don't know how, but I will choose to trust in You Lord.* I am sure that I am not the only one holding on to all I have. Can you think of a few things you haven't handed over yet? One of the things I am working on is letting our daughters go and trusting God's perfect plan for them. He gently reminds me that He loves them more than I possibly could and wants what is best for them. He sees, He knows, and He cares.

I remember a season in my life when I would come to Him in prayer asking, "Lord why does something bad always seem to happen with my family?" or "I am so tired of the struggles." Then a gentle response to my prayer was *Lisa you are missing me, I have been revealing myself to you and working things out for your good, however you are so stuck on the disappointments, therefore you are missing me. Look for Me, instead of the problems!* Since then I am looking through a different set of glasses and I see God working things out for my family. I had grown impatient because I was so focused on watching God working situations out for others, that I totally missed Him working things out for our family.

We can trust in the process and expect a solution or even a miracle. Dig your heels in and expect God to show up even in the darkest and saddest of places. God has the authority and power to do so. He is there and He wants what is best for you. We don't want a quick fix, we want a total healing.

There Is A Plan

God can and will provide for us in many ways. There are three ways He uses to encourage and inspire us to change. The first way is in community. We have one another to encourage and pray for each other. We begin to realize everyone has a story to be heard, full of ups and downs, triumphs and disappointments. In these stories we can help one another find God. From there God can do His good works in us. "For where two or three gather in my name, there am I with them" (Matthew 18:20).

The second way we will be inspired is through the Word of God. "God's Word is alive and active, and sharper than any double-edged sword, it penetrates even to dividing soul and spirit, joints and marrow; it judges the thoughts and attitudes of the heart" (Hebrew 4:12). The Bible was written by various authors over 2000 years ago and is still relevant for us today. This is amazing news! There is no situation you are going through that the Word of God cannot penetrate. It is an important tool to help you on your journey in this life.

The third way change can happen is through prayer. Prayer can be as complicated as you make it. Prayer is a conversation with God. It is not one side where you do all of the talking, it is also listening for His response. If it has been a while since you have prayed, I want you to know it is just like exercising. You first must make up your mind to do so and then stay consistent. God has a plan for you. Before you were born, you received your gifts and talents from God. The world needs you to share your calling and your story. There are many who have never had a single conversation in their home about Jesus Christ or His gift of salvation for all. Or there is doubt that God exists or cares enough for them. Even though your story is not finished, there still is hope in the chapters of your life you have already lived. It maybe your story someone needs to hear that causes them to change and to get back up, and try again.

Reflection Questions

Question #1: When did you have a time where your patience with God was tested and why?

Question #2: Looking back, how did this testing period strengthen your faith in God and how is that increase of faith impacting your life today?

Question #3: What is one way you can let go and allow God to do His work in you that you haven't done in the past?

Chapter Four
Dive Into His Word

My mind was full of questions that only the Word of God could answer. As I began to read the Bible, I realized the depth of God's love for me. He is not disappointed in me, despite my imperfections. I no longer had to pretend to have it all together. I didn't have to cover up my imperfections to look better. I was changed and amazed by the love God had for me.

Before realizing the immense love that He has for me, I had a hardened heart. Soon I found my heart softening and I began to look at others differently. In time your heart can change and become hardened by sin without God's Word there to soften you. When you let your guard down and get into the Word of God, He comes in and softens your hardened heart. Once I dived into Scripture, I found my perceptions of others softening along with my heart; I was no longer so critical or judgmental of those around me. It was like God was doing some major cardiac work on my heart and making it pump with His love and compassion.

Before God's Word, my thoughts were not His thoughts.

Just As You Are

After studying His ways I began to look at situations and people the way He would. I remember when I would walk with my friend, Val. I admired her love for Jesus and how she would freely share about Him in our conversations. Val wasn't afraid to talk about Jesus and how He was in every situation. She had studied the Word of God for years. Whenever I had a question, I would go to her to find a Scripture verse or to get her perspective. The conversations with Val, and diving in to God's Word, would cause me to ponder and grow in both who I was as a person and who I am in God's Kingdom.

One area I saw growth in was in my relationships with my family and my friends. It seemed I would often get caught up in drama whether my own or that of others. In looking back, I recognized that I wanted to be the problem solver. However I noticed that they didn't take my advice and I would become easily offended. Val taught me that the best thing I could do for those I cared about was to pray for them and their situation.

Another area I was beginning to notice a difference was in my wants and desires of worldly things. I use to think that once I had these things (such as a new home, a certain amount of money in our checking account, or a promotion), then I would be happy. The list went on and on. It didn't take long to recognize even after accomplishing or receiving a few of these things, I still felt empty. My heart was restless; not for things, but for God. I found myself thinking differently and began desiring what *God* wanted for me, not just what *I* wanted for me.

Authenticity

The beautiful thing about studying the Word with others, is that you get to be you. You don't have to be the version of you that society tells you to be or who you think you have to be, but your true, authentic self that God has made you to be. When I study the Word with others, I enjoy all the relationships that develop with those around me. Why? Because they're real. They're authentic. When we gather, we don't have to hide our inadequacies or weaknesses, we just get to be who God designed us to be. Who we are isn't designated by our faults and failures, but instead how we rise above them and use those obstacles to draw closer to Christ. These authentic relationships have been the most cherished and beautiful to me. I want to be the real deal; it is easier to keep up being real than to lie about myself and who I am.

God's Word

God is the author of Sacred Scripture. Man may have done the technical work but it was God who did the heavy lifting. It was God's Will that the Scriptures be written, so by the power of the Holy Spirit, he inspired man to make it so. You could say God was the (Holy) Ghostwriter of the Bible. The author's made the Bible come to life, but it was God who breathed life into the Bible. Because of this, we can safely say that the stories and accounts that are in the Bible, are all there because God wanted them to be. He handpicked each author of the Bible to convey the information he wanted conveyed; nothing more, nothing less. He didn't choose multiple authors for the sake of avoiding writer's cramp, but because of their different personalities, writing styles, and life journeys. Just like us all having something different to offer, so did the author's of the Bible. But even with all of these different personalities, the writings are still inspired by God and powered through the Holy Spirit. (2 Timothy 3:16).

In today's world people are in search of truth. It is through this search for truth they may ask questions like, "Is God real?" or "What proof do you have?" Our proof is the Bible. While the Bible was being penned, there is mention of the historical events taking place and of well known people that we read about in today's history books. These historical facts are the very foundation of Scripture and God's certainty. Our very essence of biblical faith is found within these historical events.

Transformation

The Bible differs from regular books because we gain divine insight of the world and predictability of the future. When you read the Bible, you can't help

Dive Into His Word

but know God. Have you ever experienced a time where you were struggling with something so you opened the Bible and a certain Scripture verse pops out and resonates with you? Moments like this are God directly guiding you. Psalm 139 talks about how God knew us before we were born. The same God that breathed inspiration into the words of Sacred Scripture knows you. He cares for you. He loves you. He wants to talk with you and knows what you need even before you ask of it. The Bible is a conversation from God to us.

"Whatever is true, whatever is noble, whatever is right, whatever is pure, whatever is lovely, whatever is admirable—if anything is excellent or praiseworthy— think about such things." (Philippians 4:8). God's Word causes us to think as He does and leads us to the right way of living. As our way of thinking changes, we find ourselves being called to action. Sometimes after reading God's Word, I am so moved by what I've read that it brings me to tears and it makes me feel so close to Him. Other times I may think of someone in particular and feel compelled to call them or send them words of encouragement. Or I may find myself feeling rebuked for saying harsh words in a conversation I had previously with a coworker or family member. It is through these actions that the Word of God can become transformational. The Word is alive, meaning it has life within it. "The Spirit gives life; the flesh counts for nothing. The words I have spoken to you— they are full of the Spirit and life." (John 6:63).

Just As You Are

You cannot help but be changed after regularly studying the Bible. Ephesians clarifies how we change by taking off our old selves and are being made new in the attitude of our mind. By putting on the new self, created to be like God, righteous and holy. (Ephesians 4:22-24). The Word of God will change and transform your heart with God's divine truths. The real truth found throughout the pages in the Bible will set you free. The supernatural power of this Book can dramatically change and transform who you are, and will be able to live out the true meaning of your life. God reveals to us how He wants us to live, and the plans He has for us. You will grow in knowledge of God which will grow your personal relationship with Him. The more knowledge you gain about God, Jesus and the Holy Spirit, the stronger and deeper your relationship will become with them. Just like any relationship you are in, the more you begin to know the person, the more you can relate to them. The relationship grows and flourishes, so it is with our Lord.

The Word of God will change the way you live and behave. I always said that once the Word is in your bone and marrow it is a life altering experience. Before I started out on this journey, I did not realize the impact it would have in my personal life. I started out just wanting to be in a women's Bible study for my own personal reasons. I never thought of the impact this one Bible study would have on my family and those I would come in contact with. It was as if God unleashed His flame within me to go out and evangelize. There was no desire to turn back, I only wanted more. The Lord is first in my life and the one I run to for everything good or bad. I only wish I would have started attending Bible studies when I was younger. But instead of regrets, I am choosing to trust in God's perfect timing. The moral of the story? It is never to early or late to begin reading the Bible.

Praying With The Word

When I am consistent with reading Scripture; my prayer life becomes richer and fuller. The first step in getting into a consistent routine is to keep it simple. I would like to share with you a simple application of combining prayer and Scripture. A friend of mine Fr. Pete, introduced me to the beauty of praying with the Psalms. He said he often would place himself in the Psalms, read them slowly, and reflect on them. He said it was his favorite way to pray so I thought that I would like to give it a try. I, too, found the Psalms were inspiring and provided me with some amazing prayer opportunities.

This is how I pray with the Psalms; at the beginning of each Psalm is a subtitle of the chapter. The chapters list numerous circumstances of life. Whatever the circumstance, I can find a Psalm to address my need. Once I find the Psalm, I imagine myself going to God as I pray the Psalm. I insert my name into the places it pertains. The prayer that comes out by doing this is real and authentic. I am reminded that God is there in all seasons of my life, whether it is in the struggles or in the praises and thanksgiving. I apply the same applications when I pray for others and their situations.

I remember the days of studying God's Word, and how I had tried to read the Bible as a book. I was not inspired at all by treating the Bible in this way. I ultimately found that using a Bible study on a specific book has given me the greatest inspiration for discernment and journaling.

Here are some more practical ways you can begin studying God's Word.

•Don't do it alone. I found out when I was trying to do it alone it was not as fruitful as it could have been through discussions with others. It was getting other's perspectives that became so invaluable to me.

•There are a couple of resources that I have found useful when it comes to studying the Bible. They are a Bible Dictionary and a Bible Commentary.

•Start out with Bible studies that not only give you Theology but help you to piece it together with your own life situations. Because of my zeal for Scripture, I was inspired to write Bible studies. *Rise Up, Women of God*, which is a Scripture study on 1 John and 2 John, and *Simply,* a women's bible study on Ecclesiastes. Both of these studies will give you some practical ways to apply the Scriptures to your everyday life.

Dive Into His Word

•Set a goal to start out small. Begin with studies that will help guide you to inspiration by the Holy Spirit. If you go solely for the education in heavy based Theology, you may lose interest or feel overwhelmed. Your zeal to learn more will come after you have met the Lord Jesus Christ in His Word.

Every good idea begins with a decision. Once the decision is made, the second hurdle is to become committed. Remember when I said that I made the commitment to start my day with God? When I was challenged to get up early in the morning, I would use the excuse that my young children were not sleeping through the night. Granted, sleep is important however spending time with God would help me to become a better person. Because of the time spent in prayer I was able to get through the day in a better frame of mind no matter what would come my way.

Once you start, stay with it and be consistent. Research suggests that it takes twenty-one days to form a good or bad habit. So, when you read the Word of God, try to find a groove and stick with it for a consecutive twenty-one days to form a habit. You will see the fruits in doing so and your days will go much better because you did.

Reflection Questions

Question #1: When was a time that you read Scripture and it spoke directly to your heart? What was the Scripture?

Question #2: How have you seen God's Word impact your attitude during your day-to-day life?

Question #3: What are the biggest roadblocks to getting into the Word on a daily basis? How can you overcome this hurdle? What do you need to change in order to make getting into the Word a habit?

Chapter Five
Get Into His Community

I recall that big move after my husband's promotion. We had just finished building our home and the family was adjusting to their new environment. During the day I would be home alone in this new town because I hadn't yet found a way to get involved in our new community. However, shortly after moving, our neighbor, Amy, began stopping by to visit. What inspired me about Amy was her joy and commitment to her church and to her women's Bible study. After listening to her, there would be a hunger inside of me for such a life! What I wanted was God to light my heart on fire the way He did for Amy. I no longer wanted to be lukewarm or bored with my faith. I hungered to meet Him in His Word and wanted to make sense out of my life.

I am an introvert at heart so I hadn't felt comfortable to invite myself to the study back then. I was insecure about my lack of knowledge on how to use the Bible. So, I did what any desperate woman would do. I took it to prayer! I asked God to put it on Amy's heart to invite me to the women's Bible study.

Just As You Are

A few weeks after that prayer, Amy stopped by my house and invited me to join her Bible study group. When I think back, this one prayer that God answered through Amy has changed my life. Prayer is powerful. I confessed to Amy my insecurities and as well as my longing to learn and be a part of a Bible study. I asked her what I needed to have on hand and she gave me the study book. My first study was a Beth Moore study, *A Heart Like His.* It was a study on John. I couldn't have chosen a better Gospel to start with, can you? It was as if God wanted to meet me through this study in such a profound way. I could hardly wait.

In my first Bible study group there were twelve to fifteen women. We were a diverse group of married, single, widowed, young, mature, and multi-denominational women from all walks of life. The conversations were lively and beautifully comprised of trials and triumphs. The women were kind, respectful, and nonjudgmental. Not once did I feel badly because I was new to studying the Bible.

The impact these women had on me was profound in so many ways. I was in a sales career and had learned how to network with others in order to build a team to grow my business. Because of this, I knew quite a few people throughout the country. What I began to realize is that some of the connections were not authentic and admittedly, I wasn't always authentic with them in return. It was as if we were friends only because we wanted or needed something. But the

Get Into His Community

women from my Bible study group were different. For the first time, no one wanted anything from me and there was nothing I wanted from them. I had found true authentic friendships. When God placed it on my heart to pray for an invitation to a Bible study, it was as if He veered me off my course to a path that led me straight to Him. This experience changed my life by renewing my faith and giving me a richer relationship with Him. That one study would be a life-altering event for me and my family.

Your life with community will be full and secure because we are called to be there for one another. In a healthy community, you can count on one another for support and prayer. In the community I had found, we would ask each other for prayer requests and intentions, so we knew specifically how to pray for one another that following week. The comfort I felt knowing someone else was praying for my intentions was powerful and I found myself fulfilled in praying for others and their intentions. As we would talk about our lives, I would be astounded by the joy the others had even while talking about their trials. This led me to discover how one can have joy within the struggle. This type of joy comes from being in God's word and expecting He is with you no matter what is happening in your life.

In today's day and age, diversity tends to be looked down upon. But when it comes to your community, diversity can be a good and beautiful thing. It helps us to expand what we know and are comfortable with. Of course, there are those who you will relate to more than others but I encourage you to step out of your comfort zone. When I think about God connecting the dots for the community, I could see Him placing us together in order to bear fruit. Once in a while we would have visitors who would stop by to check us out. There were times when friends or relatives of our group would be visiting, and instead of skipping the study we brought them along. It was a great example of how important it was to us to gather together and study the Word of God.

Community Matters

Sometimes in my shyness I am tempted to keep to myself but when I isolate myself from others, I am not sharing my gifts and talents; I am keeping them hidden. When we are insecure or unsure, fear sets in. Fear is not from God. Satan is the master of excuse and wants to give you a reason to hold you back from studying the Bible. Even though I was embarrassed about not knowing much about the Bible, I knew I couldn't let the insecurity I was feeling keep me from God's Word. When you are not a part of a community, it is easy to experience isolation and the effects of loneliness just as I had when my first husband died. As humans we yearn for interactions with others, and just as the Trinity is communal, we are called to be the same.

God is a relational God. He longs for community with

us. In Scripture, the value of community is displayed in Hebrews, "And let us consider how we may spur one another on toward love and good deeds, not giving up meeting together, as some are in the habit of doing, but encouraging one another—and all the more as you see the Day approaching." (Hebrews 10:24-25). This is a perfect example of a solid community. You will be blessed to have these authentic relationships in your life. When you look to others for advice, look to those who love you and have your best interest in mind. I remember being surprised by other's responses when I told them I was joining a Bible study group and it made me wonder if I should go through with it. But I felt the Lord calling me to do it, so I stayed firm in my resolve.

Finding A Community

To find a community, begin with prayer. Ask God to help you find the right group. When you are focused, God has a way of revealing to you what you need. In your search, you will want to make sure the group you are considering is not exclusive. One of the most destructive forces of a small group is this sense that you are not welcome. Unfortunately, there are cliques in the Christian communities and they are not as inviting. As you are searching, if you come upon a group like this, you will know this is not a healthy community to surround yourself with.

Begin a conversation with your pastor regarding your

search for a small group. The pastor may know of a small group you could look into. From there listen to conversations among your coworkers, friends, and family. You would be amazed how many people publicly share about their small groups. I had such a situation happen when I was waiting for my hair stylist. I overheard her talking to someone about a study she did and I found out she was in my neighborhood. I said something and she invited me to join her study!

Be attentive to the Holy Spirit because He has your best interests in mind. God will lead you in the right direction because He wants what is best for you. There are no coincidences with God; there are only opportunities waiting for you. Because I had a relationship with my friend Amy, I trusted her. Because I knew her, I was able to be honest about my insecurities when it came to the Bible. She wasn't judgmental which showed me I would be in a healthy community. Let the Holy Spirit help you discern if it is the right fit for you. If it isn't a good fit don't be afraid to leave and search for another group. If you cannot find one, decide if you want to start a small group yourself. If you don't feel ready, see if there is someone you know that has experience leading small groups that might be willing to help you get a small group started.

The purpose of a small group is to encourage, affirm, and pray for one another, to help one another grow in their journey with Christ, and to help one another in their time of need. I have been in groups of twelve and in groups of three and have found six to eight people to be ideal. Sometimes if groups are too big, it can be difficult for everyone to share their thoughts due to time constrictions. A large group may be a good indication that it is time to break into smaller groups and regrow by inviting others to join you. If a group is too small, there isn't much diversity and one person's absence could make it an even smaller group for the day. If your group is small, keep working to grow and expand. You never know who is in need of your small group.

Like prayer, the Word brings us together and activates our faith. When we study together, it helps us to get a different perspective on the reactions others have when they read the same Scripture. God speaks to each of us differently because He knows our hearts. When different people join together in prayer, they have the opportunity to build authentic relationships with those they are praying with. These relationships can turn into unexpected friendships. And even for this introvert, I have found that life is more fun when you can do it together. I have attended Christian conferences and retreats, gone hiking, and had dinner with those friends that I met within my small groups, all of whom I probably wouldn't have gotten to know otherwise. We enjoy each other's company and the authentic friendships that have been created through prayer.

Reflection Questions

Question #1: What are the most significant and the most practical ways that community has impacted your life?

Question #2: Have you ever had times of isolation? When was it and why? What were the effects of isolation on your life?

Question #3: If you are a small group, who could you invite to join you? If you are not, how could you take the first step in joining one? Either way, what would your prayer be?

Chapter Six
Answer His Calling

How you see yourself matters. *Mirror, mirror on the wall, I don't like ...* Can you think of some things you may have said to yourself as you stared in the mirror? It is easy to be complementary to others but we're much more critical of ourselves. I had not realized the negative self-talk I had been having until it came time for me to record a Bible series session. I had pleaded with God to help me with this obstacle. As I was looking in the mirror one morning I said, "God, you are going to receive a worn-out bride by the time I get there." I remember laughing quietly when a rebuke came to my heart. *Are you saying I messed up? When you do not like what you see, basically you think I have messed up. You tell people how perfect and wonderful I am then why would I mess up? You think you look worn out but it is the opposite. I see you trying to become a righteous person, therefore in my eyes, instead of looking old and worn out, you are looking radiant. I the Lord am making you new.*

The rebuke from the Lord inspired me to write this book. God gave me a visual of a bride facing the bridegroom, in her wedding dress, with the front of the gown radiant and glowing whereas the back of the dress was gray and the hem was all tattered and dingy. The front of the person in the dress knew God and heard His voice and their life changed for the good. The back side represented the past life without God.

Identity

The source of your identity is critical because the world is more than willing to tell you who you are, but remember, you are not of this world. You were created in the image and likeness of God. Your value is not in what you do, how much money you have, the titles following your name, or your past. You are somebody and you are a big deal! "For you are his handiwork created in Christ Jesus for the good works that God has prepared in advance, that we should live in them." (Ephesians 2:10)

You see before you were born, God had a specific purpose for you; one of goodness and love. Sounds so simple doesn't it? However it is anything but simple in our world today. From the time you begin school you become infiltrated with what the secular world wants your identity to be. Secular is defined as without God, so be careful who you listen to.

You may think you are not enough but God says you are perfect in every way. When God created the universe, He desired to create man and female. "Then God said,

Answer His Calling

"Let us make man in our image, in our likeness, so that they may rule over the fish in the sea and the birds in the sky, over the livestock and all the wild animals, and over all the creatures that move along the ground." So God created mankind in his own image, in the image of God he created them; male and female he created them." (Genesis 1:26-27). Did you see it? You were made in His own image and likeness. Therefore you are beautiful and are lacking nothing.

Satan is afraid you may realize your worth and value. If you buy Satan's lie, you are no longer a threat to him. Therefore, it is important to get this right before we finish this study. You are beautiful and wonderfully made. Receive it and remind yourself that God held nothing back when He created you. The secular world will try to convince you of the opposite, but I want you to quit listening to the secular world. I give you permission today to say NO. You are no longer of this world, you are becoming new.

We are not alone in our struggles as one can look around and see there are many others who are unsure of who they are. There is so much brokenness in our world because there are many who have bought the lie. Can you see why Christianity seems to be in a crisis? We must figure out who we are and who God created us to be.

From the time you are in high school, people will begin to advise you on what educational degree will bring you financial success. The thought of God and His plan for your does not enter your mind. Your dreams are caught up in what the world has flashed in front of you. You begin to set standards of what success looks like to you. The world tells you that your worth is found in what others think and their expectations. of you; 'If you want to be somebody, you must climb the ladder to success'. Because of the desire to make it to the top, sometimes budgets are pushed off to the side and debt is on the rise. People have put the ability to be instantly rewarded above the ability to save purposefully. From there we begin to use people because they may be able to help us get to the next step. We find ourselves ignoring those who can't help us and begin to think we are superior above others.

In God's opinion, you are significant enough that He sent His only Son to come in the flesh and die on the cross for your salvation. (John 3:16). This is how big of a deal you are. Your life affects more people than you may realize.

Your Story

Your story matters because it may be the narrative a person needs to hear to keep going or to turn to God. We all have struggles. It's not a matter of if, it is only a matter of when. When the storm arises, your story may be the one to encourage someone to hang on and cling to Jesus. You are valuable because God loves you and created you for such a time as this.

Answer His Calling

The same God who knows the number of hairs on your head, wants to fellowship with you. So don't be afraid; you are worth more than many sparrows. (Matthew 10:30-31).

God tells you to find your worth in His truth. Where do we find His truth? In the Bible. For those who receive Him into their lives, are God's children through adoption, and our identity becomes as a son or daughter of God. "See what great love the Father has lavished on us, that we should be called children of God! And that is what we are! The reason the world does not know us is that it did not know him." (1 John 3:1).

Have you ever thought of why you were born at this time? Why you live where you live? God has placed you here at this time in the place you call home to serve Him and bring Him glory. I know you have a testimony because each of us has a defining moment in our lives where we either choose to stay stuck or we turn to Christ for his assistance to overcome the situation. Your story matters and has impact because there is someone who needs to hear it. Your story has the potential to be a blessing to those who have come to Christ, and to those who do not know Christ. The Bible is full of individuals who came to Christ with their situations and they were saved and walked away changed. It is their very stories that inspire me to trust that God is with me and He will help me and will never let go of me. God is ready to do His part; are you ready to do yours by sharing your story?

Just As You Are

Occasionally, I hear people compare their testimony to mine and say that their story isn't as dramatic as mine. I am here to say *praise be Jesus* that it isn't. If the end result of your story led you to Jesus, then your end result is just as important as mine. You see, that is all that matters because God cares about each and every soul and your story may be the one to turn them to Jesus. "What do you think? If a man owns a hundred sheep, and one of them wanders away, will he not leave the ninety-nine on the hills and go to look for the one that wandered off? And if he finds it, truly I tell you, he is happier about that one sheep than about the ninety-nine that did not wander off. In the same way your Father in heaven is not willing that any of these little ones should perish." (Matthew 18:12-14). You can see that God does not look at numbers like we are accustomed to. I remember a valuable lesson I had learned as a new youth minister. I had the best laid plans to launch a successful ministry. The one concern I had with my plan was that I had no control over whether the youth would come. I remember the words of my pastor; "Lisa I am not concerned about the numbers; my concern is with the souls". Then he reminded me that the battle was the Lords. As long as I prayed for them and did my best to prepare, the outcome would be in God's hands. To this day my pastor's words have been my guide and they should be your guide as well. God is looking for a willing heart to pray and prepare their story. The impact of your story to whomever shall hear it will be in God's hands.

Reflection Questions

Question #1: If you had to describe yourself in three words, what would those three words be? Are those words true? Are they God's words?

Question #2: If God had to describe you in three words, what do you think He would select?

Question #3: How could you integrate God's words about you into your identity? What would you need to do?

PART THREE
SHARING

Chapter Seven
When I First Shared

A couple of years following my first Bible study, I met up with a youth minister who asked me to lead Bible studies in two parishes that he was working for. Dave had heard about me from my hair stylist who had a Bible study in my neighborhood. She had explained how I was in another group studying the *Purpose Driven Life*. Dave had heard about the book and wanted to meet up with me. Even though I had never known Dave before, we hit it off right away because we both liked to talk about Jesus. The opportunity came up to share my story about Shane to Dave and I was not prepared for how the story would affect him. Because of his reaction, I began to realize there was power and significance in people's testimony.

Because my heart was on fire for the Lord, I wanted to serve God. I had the opportunity to do so with youth in my church. As I mentioned in the previous chapter, I had prepared and prayed for the youth who would attend. However, in the beginning months of our time together, I was having a hard time connecting with them. It was then that I felt a tug on my heart indicating that it was time to share my story with them. So I planned a night to include my testimony, worship, and adoration. As the night was approaching, there were so many things I began to think about such as the vulnerability of sharing a part of my life to the youth, the volunteers and my pastor. I was concerned that I would be an emotional mess because I hadn't shared in a big group setting before. As the time grew nearer, I suddenly realized that two of the youth who would be at this event would be Pat's and my two daughters. They had no idea about my life before their dad, so I sat them down and shared with them about life with Shane. Our daughters were amazingly calm as I was sharing my story with them. The only question they had for me is if Pat was their dad and I assured them that he was. At dinner that night, I explained how I felt called by God to share my story with the youth. Pat asked what I would be sharing. I began to wonder if I had told him everything about Shane and his visions. So I explained how I was going to share about Shane's visions and the big ball of light that went over my car. He asked if he could come and listen to my testimony and I told him I would appreciate his encouragement and support.

On the day of the event, I was nervous and second guessing myself. I began to question how my story could help anyone and whether I wanted this out there for everyone. I also realized that my pastor didn't know anything about my story which added to my nervousness. I decided to arrive ahead of my family so I could pray and read over my testimony before everyone else came. As the events of that evening began, we started off with praise and worship music and then it was time for me to share. I opened up with prayer and began to give them my story. I could tell everyone was captivated by what I said which was somewhat unnerving to me. I would glance over at our daughters Alisha and Rebecca and then Pat to see how they were doing. Once I finished, we closed in prayer and the silence was deafening. The doubts were pouring into my mind like asking God what I had done and whether I did the right thing. Our pastor stood up, thanked me for sharing, and the subsequent response from people was overwhelming. The youth and volunteers came up to me asking questions, sharing how they were inspired, or were rendered speechless and just offered hugs. All of my fears and doubts about sharing had disappeared.

Once my family and I were home from sharing my story that night, I asked them how they were doing because I was worried about them. I wanted them to know how much I loved them and to reassure them of their importance to me. We were having a snack and talking about the night when Pat told me there was more to my story. I looked at him confused because I didn't think I had left anything out. He then began sharing the story of what happened to him on the day of Shane's accident.

Pat was a highway patrolman and had been out patrolling the roads until 4 a.m. on the day of the accident. Pat explained that he would hang his uniform on the door just in case the police scanner went off and he was called out. A call for assistance did go out that day; a request for help at my ranch. After he heard the call, Pat got up and went to the door to grab his uniform when something told him to sit back down. He was told Shane had died and that he was to take care of me. He didn't quite know what it meant so he grabbed his uniform and quickly got dressed. He knew the ambulance was already in route to the hospital so he had stopped by the church and told Father Rich, "There has been an accident and Lisa needs you. Come and I will take you to the hospital". Pat was the highway patrolman standing at the nurse's station when Shane's dad and brother took me to the room Shane was in.

It was my turn to have my jaw drop as I heard Pat's story. My mind was racing as I heard more details of the intertwining story and I didn't know what to think. I wondered how Pat knew that Shane was the one that the ambulance had been called for. So, I asked Pat if the information was given on the police scanner and he replied that they hadn't shared who was hurt. I had always wondered how Fr. Rich knew about the accident and was there at the hospital for me and now I understood the stunning truth: my story had more pages to it than I could have even imagined. Pat would wonder about the story from that day on. In doing so, he would remember even more details about that day and share them with me. From then on whenever I was asked to share my testimony and Pat was with me, I would always stop and ask Pat to come up and share his part of the story. One such night after I was done sharing my part, Pat went and stood in front of the alter during adoration and began giving his portion of the testimony. When he came to the part about being told to sit down, of Shane's death, and the instruction to take care of me, his knees almost gave out and he looked stunned. As I wondered if he was okay, Pat composed himself and said, "You know, I hadn't gone to church much prior to meeting Lisa because I felt uncomfortable to go to church by myself, and this is why; I couldn't recognize the voice until now. The message I was given was from God!" Pat continued, "You see, Shane shared with Lisa that he loved Jesus and felt close to Him. Maybe this is why Shane had those visions. Maybe we, too, could know more if our relationship with Jesus was better and we paid attention to God and all that is going on around us."

Pat still thinks about the events of the horse accident as well as the events that are going on in our lives looking for God. A few years later, Pat was reflecting on Shane's visions and remembered that on the day of the airplane crash, he and his brother were driving the truck and drove to the scene of the plane crash from Shane's vision. Pat was beginning to piece together all the ways God had brought us together. He even pieced together the details that both of our paternal grandmothers, the only living grandparents, were both devout Catholics and were each from towns named Fairfax in two different states.

During this time, our family was on fire for Christ

and we were all hungry to grow in our faith. A couple of years had passed when, and we were on our way to church, God had put the idea of moving on my heart. I was nervous because I was happy with where we were living, loved what I did, and wasn't especially sure about leaving the place that our family had grown the most in our spirituality. As I was mulling these thoughts over, we come upon a stoplight when, out of the blue, my husband said, "You know, I am ready to retire from my job." I took a deep breath and thought to myself, *Are you crazy? We have two daughters getting ready to go off to college!* As soon as that thought entered my head, I was reminded once again that God would be with us. After church, a friend came up to me and asked if the Lord was doing something with me and my family. I told her I think He may be calling us to move. She said she had been wondering about the same thing. From that point on, I knew I would need to pray and listen for God and what He was calling us to do. After some time I shared with the family about what God had placed on my heart, and three months later, Pat retired from his job.

The girls forged ahead making plans to attend college in the fall as I looked for a ministry job. I had made contact with a former neighbor of ours who was a deacon and he told me there was a youth minister opening at a church in his area. A few days after talking with the pastor, I met up with him for an interview. He called me the following day to offer me the job if I was still interested. Our deacon friend

When I First Shared

had talked to a realtor in the area who called with a
house for us to look at. I was excited and thought,
'Wow this must be God's plan. Everything's coming
together! We'll be in the same town as our daughters
while they're going to college, we'll be closer to Pat
and my family, we have a lot of friends in this area, I
have a job and now a possible new home!' However,
even with all these things in our favor, there was
one thing I was still missing; peace. I had no peace
about moving to the new area or working at my new
job offer, and for the life of me I could not figure
out why. I talked with my pastor and he suggested
that I take a week to pray and think about it. During
this time, I received a call from another pastor who
was on the other end of the state. He wanted me to
consider talking to him about a campus and youth
ministry job. My heart was in turmoil because I didn't
want to give up all the perks of the first location
even though I knew I was not feeling called there. I
remember saying to my husband, "There is no way
on God's green earth we will move to the other end
of the state." However, I knew that if I wanted to
be obedient to God, I would at least listen to what
the pastor had to say. I had undeniable peace after
visiting with him, so the decision our family chose
was to be obedient to God. We were going to trust in
the Lord's plan and move to a town on the opposite
end of the state from our girls, family, and friends. It
was a chaotic time with me adjusting to a new job
at one end of the state, the girls at the other end
starting college, and my husband back at our prior
home trying to sell it and pack. Despite all of this, I

still had peace about the decision.

In three years' time, both of our girls transferred to different universities, my husband was working part time at the same church as I, and we were seeing the fruits of our labor with the youth and college students. But just when we became comfortable, a new Pastor was assigned to our church and things begin to change for the worse. Heartache and tears became a regular part of my day and I began to second guess our decision. I wondered why God led us here, away from all the things we had desired. After many trials and hardships, I sought direction from another pastor. He said, "Lisa, I want to thank you and your family for your sacrifices because you may not hear these words from anyone else. Those you served are better because of your willingness to give up everything for the Lord's call. However, I am concerned that you and your family will lose your faith. Is there another church you can go to as you are discerning what the Lord wants you to do?" We began to go to a church outside of our area and Pat began to look for a full-time job just in case things fell through for me at the church. Pat soon found employment and after continuing to struggle with my job, I felt that God had finally released me and said I could go. Even with the pain I was going through, it was a hard decision because I loved ministering to the youth and the college students and, while I didn't want to leave them, I knew it was no longer good for me to stay.

When I First Shared

Then, after four months of feeling lost and hurt, I made a call to a pastor in our area and asked him if he would give me spiritual direction. At one of our meetings, the pastor asked me what I felt God was calling me to do and I blurted out, "I think I am supposed to write Bible studies, but who will think I have any credibility to do such a thing?" He said, "Lisa, stop for I am concerned with which voice you are listening to." I was stunned by his words. He continued on, "Who gives you your desires to write?" I answered, "God." He then asked, "Who is the voice telling you no one would want them or would be critical of them?" I said, "Well it isn't from God." He said, "That is right." He then told me to go home and study Genesis 12 for the next two weeks and reflect on how God had called Abraham to leave his family and all that he was familiar with to serve God's plans.

Meanwhile, we had a new pastor assigned to our church. His name was Father Pete. He made the Word of God come alive and would use unorthodox props for his sermons such as fishing gear, a mining pick, or an art easel. Fr. Pete was on fire and brought my faith, and that of my family, back to life. He kept hinting to me that he wanted me to lead the middle and high school youth of our church. I have to confess that I was nervous about working for the church again but after eight months of hinting, he asked if he could come to our home for supper. Fr. Pete got right to the point and asked me to help him build the youth in our church. Although I was still hesitant, a couple of weeks later I said I would.

Just As You Are

On my first day of work, he asked me to come by for lunch. When I arrived, he was baking bread and pointed to two cans of soup sitting on the counter. He gave me instructions to take those two cans of soup and begin doctoring it up with whatever I could find in the cupboard or refrigerator. As I was stirring the soup, he began to set the table for eight people who would be joining us for lunch. All I could think was that Fr. Pete expected a miracle to happen with only two cans of soup and a loaf of bread! As God would have it, we had enough food and the conversations that took place around the table that day were exhilarating. As I was helping him clean up, I shared with Fr. Pete that I felt God wanted me to write a Bible study. Fr. Pete challenged me to write one and present it to a group of women from our church. I became inspired by what I had witnessed that I came home and wrote a blog "The Soup Can Ministry." I was so thankful God gave us Fr. Pete.

Two weeks later, it was Thanksgiving. We had given Fr. Pete an invitation to spend the day with us at our cabin. Although he hadn't given us a definite answer, we were ready for him. When he didn't attend, we attributed it to him having another engagement. A few nights later, I attempted to call Fr. Pete and confirm details for a dinner that was planned with four young adult women. After not hearing from him, I decided that he had probably figured it out and we'd just see what happens. Once we arrived at the church, we found a note on the door stating there would be no services for the evening. I told

When I First Shared

my family that something was not right and sadly, I was right. After talking to the secretary of our church, we found out Fr. Pete had gone for a ride in his airplane and had not come back. A search and rescue team eventually discovered his plane which had crashed over some mountains. Once again I began to question God as to why something like this would happen. A short time later, I realized why God had placed me at this church. Shortly after Fr. Pete's funeral, a counselor was sent to our church to meet up with the three of us who worked there. Basically, the counselor was sent to help us with our grief and further instructed us to be the rock for the church members during the Advent and Christmas season until a new pastor could be assigned after the first of the new year.

It was a sad season and at the start of the new year, I couldn't shake the conversation Fr. Pete and I had about me writing a Bible study and testing it out on the women of our church. So I felt compelled to follow through and began to write my first Bible study on 1 John and 2 John. It was a challenging and an exciting experience that provided me much healing after everything that had happened since our move to the area. Since that time, I've continued to serve as a youth minister at our church and have written additional Bible studies and blogs. I am involved with a national church resource and lead retreats for youth on up. I firmly believe that had we not moved this third time, I wouldn't have started my writing career. God took me out of my comfort zone so that He could grow me more and give me deeper roots. God once again showed me that something beautiful can come out of something devastating and broken.

The Impact of A Testimony

By sharing my testimony, it seemed conversations about life and Jesus would naturally happen. Our daughters were asking questions about their faith, especially when they were struggling with something. They would often tell me that they don't know how I handled all that I went through at only twenty-two years of age. It was because of my testimony they found the strength and courage to face their challenges and struggles. The impact on my husband following the testimony gave him the desire to jump on board and join a men's Bible study. The men would meet once a week at 6 a.m. and study the Word of God. Following one of the studies, my husband came home and said, "I told the guys that your goal is Heaven and that I needed to catch up because I want the same thing." Pat wanted to share his passion for Jesus and began to volunteer in ministry opportunities for both the youth and men. When we moved to our current home, he began a men's study group. These men meet in a lumberyard at 6 a.m. every week to study the Word of God.

God uses my testimony to this day and encourages and inspires people that no matter what life brings their way they are never alone. My hope is that when I share the testimony, people leave knowing that God is with them no matter the struggle and they can trust in his plan for them.

Your story matters and there are people who are waiting to hear your story. You may never know the implications your story could have on someone's life. If your story points them to God, then you can know you have served the Lord well. It is time to see how to start a fire and fan the flame.

Reflection Questions

Question #1: What is your testimony? Have you shared it with anyone? What do you think would happen if you shared it more often?

Question #2: Why do you think every testimony matters, both large and small?

Question #3: What Scripture supports the sharing of testimony? Can you find three of them to give you the confidence and assurance to share your testimony?

Chapter Eight
Start A Fire

"**A**nd you also must testify, for you have been with me from the beginning." (John 15:27) All of us are called to give our testimony of when God entered into our lives. When we give our testimony, we reveal the true and living God to those around us. God uses our stories to reach others' hearts in a way nothing else can. This is referred to as *Cor ad Cor Loquitur* or *Heart Speaks to Heart*. When you read the Bible, you will notice that it is not only a series of individual accounts but the personal testimonies of the authors as well. Each chapter reveals how God entered into people's hearts and their lives were changed for the better. Where would we be without this amazing Book of testimonies? When someone hears how God has been at work in your life, it can make an impact on them that may change their entire way of living.

Testimonies are inviting, because you are extending a personal invitation for others to come and enter into your story. In doing so you are opening yourself up to those listening. I am reminded of the invitation found in Revelations, "The Spirit and the bride say,

'Come' and let the one who hears say, 'Come' and let the one who is thirsty come; let the one who wishes take the water of life without cost." (Revelations 22:17) You never know who God will be sending your way. They could be thirsting for the very hope your story could offer.

It is difficult to argue with a personal experience. When a person testifies about an event that has happened in their life it can't be refuted. This reminds me of what I had discussed in Chapter Four regarding how there is proof; the Bible is real because of the historical evidence. This one fact makes it hard to disprove. Your story has the potential to impact future generations. Why not leave your story as a part of your legacy like those who went before us? Because of them, we can read their stories for encouragement and inspire others to do the same.

Testimonies are powerful because of the effects they have on people. Those who hear your story are called to action or are motivated to make a change in their life. An outpouring from their response can in turn be a blessing to others. It's as if you have given them permission by your example to go out and share their story with others. More often than not, the stories which speak to our hearts are the personal stories. Think of someone you are close to and what makes you close to them. It's more than likely that you can relate to one another and this is what it is like when you share your stories with each other. Sometimes we may think our story is insignificant but God has called you to think bigger because you are a child of God and your playing small does not suit anyone. As I mentioned earlier, you are here at this time right now for a purpose, and you were created to reveal God's salvation message to all you meet. As you are sharing your testimony with others, never doubt the greatness of God and how big your testimony may be. You do have a story and every story matters for the Kingdom of Heaven. You are His and He will give you everything necessary to share your story.

My story is not your story. You do not need a tragedy or traumatic experience to be impactful with your testimony. God will place those who need your testimony in your path to be a source of encouragement for them. A common pitfall is when you think your testimony isn't good enough. If this thought has crossed your mind, I want you to say NO to it. Remember the Devil does not want stories of truth to be told, because they could be used to help someone get to Heaven. Which story of yours needs to be told? Now is the time to take courage, be bold and be ready to share. I am reminded of the Gospel of Mark, as he instructs the people to go home and report all the great things God had done for them. (Mark 5:19). You have been given permission to do the same.

One of my favorite things is not just getting to know those I have ministered to, but getting to be a part of their lives and watch them as they go along their journey. When I receive a wedding invitation or a baby announcement I am reminded of the bond we share because of my willingness to share my story with them. You are a witness to God and called to use your story to expand His Kingdom. You have been assigned to help turn souls to Christ. It's time to ask yourself if you're going to freeze from stage fright or are you going to take a leap of faith and play your part. Every one of us faces these crossroads at some point in our lives. I hope you can be bold and courageous and play your part on the grand stage of life. I promise you will feel a sense of peace and joy that cannot be imitated. I often have people ask me why I am so positive or so happy. It isn't because I don't have problems or trials. My happiness comes from my personal relationship with Jesus. I found Him in my story, stories of others, and those in the Bible. Who do you know that needs some joy?

The impact on your church could be life giving. The more we open up our lives to one another the more we can help one another encounter Christ. This is what evangelization and discipleship is all about. "Therefore encourage one another and build one another up, just as you are doing." (1 Thessalonians 5:11) Churches have a need for people to evangelize and disciple. The most effective evangelization tool is peoples' testimony. Think about your life and where you are now. There is no way you haven't changed in one way or another. Your story needs not a major life change to inspire someone; it just needs your heart to impact people you are called to share with. The more souls reached the bigger the impact will be for the Kingdom. Your legacy could have a lasting effect for years to come. People won't know your story unless you tell it. My family has changed for the better because of all the stories we have heard or read about in the Bible. Because of the stories, our one goal in this life is Heaven.

Now Is The Time

None of us know what tomorrow will bring. We are never guaranteed years, months, days, or even moments. So why am I saying this? Because now is the time to act. Even if you have years, you may miss an opportunity because you hesitated. Each person God sends your way may be looking for the words of everlasting life for you to share with them.

While working for the city, Pat had gotten to know a man named Junior who was a World War II veteran. He was a colorful and delightful man who grew to become a family friend of ours. I knew Junior had faith but it seemed to be a gray area in his life. One day, we received the news that Junior had taken his own life; he was ninety-three years old. I realized then that I had never taken the time to share my story with him. I don't know if my story could have given Junior hope but my heart aches for him and the missed opportunity. I wish I could have another chance just to share my testimony with him. The book of Romans reminds us of why we should have a sense of urgency, "And do this, understanding the present time: The hour has already come for you to wake up from your slumber, because our salvation is nearer now than when we first believed." (Romans 13:11).

Be attuned to the Spirit and He will inspire you with the words and opportunities to speak up. I am so glad that I don't have to rely solely on myself when it comes to my testimony; God and the Holy Spirit have my back and they have yours too. I know exactly where and who my story comes from and who the ghostwriter of my testimony is. When I share my story, I pray and ask God to give me wisdom on how to go about it. When you are attuned to the Spirit, you do not have to second guess yourself.

Always be ready to share your testimony no matter where you are, because God may have someone right next to you for a reason. Because of my friend Junior, I now stand ready to share my story at a moment's notice. In 1 Peter, the Spirit instructs us that "our hearts revere Christ as Lord. Always be prepared to give an answer to everyone who asks you to give the reason for the hope that you have. But do this with gentleness and respect." (1 Peter 3:15)

I remember when our girls were young and I read them a book about how there was only one you. Every picture in the book had a fingerprint, whether it was on a butterfly or lion, to illustrate that no one else is like you. God only made one you. Take this as God's way of saying "Just be as you are, because you are enough." You matter, and your story matters. So today I give you permission to embrace yourself and remember you are beautifully and wonderfully made.

"Be who God meant you to be, and you will set the world on fire." - Catherine of Siena

Reflection Questions

Question #1: What would your prayer be in order to become more bold in sharing your testimony? How do you think King David prayed for boldness?

Question #2: What is the balance between your story being about you or about God and both of your distinct roles?

Question #3: Who will be the first person you share your story with?

Conclusion

Life is a page turner with joy and sorrows. When I said God works things out for us, I am not being naïve that we won't have to go through periods of pain as He is doing so. As a pastor once explained it to me, "Lisa as you say yes to God's plan, it's compared to Jesus' Paschal Mystery." You may ask what is the Paschal Mystery? It is dying and rising, just as Jesus did in His Passion and Resurrection of death and new life. The seasons reflect the same, such as Fall represents the dying of plants and leaves falling from the trees, to winter where everything seems complacent, awaiting for new life which is Spring. In our lives the Paschal Mystery looks like this: The first phase of the Paschal Mystery is death to yourself, your plans, and your desires. The next step is the tomb, this is where you can stay as long as you like; this is when you can be stuck in fear and doubt, or spend time with Jesus for His mercy and grace to enter into you as you make sense of things. When you are ready to move forward, you have reached the Resurrection. The Resurrection is moving forward to the next chapter of your new life in hope and trusting that God is with you. Jesus' example shows us death does not have the final say, and that there is meaning in life no matter what comes our way. There is light in the darkness, which is where your story evolves.

Have you ever looked at your life as a book? I hadn't thought about my life this way until I realized there was a definite end to a chapter with Shane. I soon found there was a new chapter full of firsts included marrying Pat, and there have been many chapters since then. One thing for certain, is each one has caused me to grow in my faith. Everyone's story begins at birth and will end at death, however a story can continue on to be shared through those you know and love. No one knows how long their story will be or how long the chapters will be in the book. God designed for you to be here at this time for a reason, and to share with others how He is working in your life, because God thought you were important enough to make your story a chapter in His story.

As you go through life, always remember that God is with you, and He will never abandon or forsake you. No matter the story you have or where you are at on your journey, hold firm to Jesus and never let go. Remember to stay in His Word and pray unceasingly. Last, be courageous and willing to set the world on fire by being just as you are.

About The Author

Lisa Fahey is an author and speaker with over twenty years of experience working with youth, adults and women in the Church. She is the author of *Rise Up Women of God, A Scripture Study on 1 John and 2 John; Simply. A Women's Study on Ecclesiastes; Simply. Advent* and soon to be released *Just As You Are, How Your Testimony Can Impact People In Ways You Never Thought Possible.* All are meant to inspire, encourage and empower readers in their journey with God. Lisa draws on a wealth of real-life stories and moments with God to inspire and encourage others.

At the young age of 21, Lisa lost her first husband and this forever changed her approach to God and His word. Through her work, she shares how God helped her to continue to grow and rise up as a woman of God even during the trials of life. Through her Bible studies, Lisa has a unique ability for helping her readers see that while "life is hard and messy, the treasure of living life to the fullest is by living it; just simply."

Just As You Are

Through her Bible studies and speaking, Lisa has something special for everyone to help encourage them in their relationship and journey with God. By carefully crafting and designing engaging, interactive and spiritually rich Bible studies, Lisa aims to help women discover their identity in God. Her goal is to help create passionate, dedicated leaders who will be the people that God and the church need them to be. Lisa has made the upliftment of others her life's calling.

Drawing on the authority of God's word and the guidance of His Spirit, Lisa leads her readers through a journey of discovery, growth and strength in Christ. Lisa has been married to her husband Pat for over thirty years and is the mother of two beautiful daughters Alisha and Rebecca. She holds her Certificate in Theology from John Paul the Great University.

For more information or to contact Lisa, visit her website: www.lisafahey.com